Yellow Umbrella Books are published by Red Brick Learning
7825 Telegraph Road, Bloomington, Minnesota 55438
http://www.redbricklearning.com

Library of Congress Cataloging-in-Publication Data
Trumbauer, Lisa.
    [What makes ten? Spanish]
    ¿Qué hace diez?/por Lisa Trumbauer.
    p. cm.
    Includes index.
    Summary: "Simple text and photos present the concept that objects can be grouped in different ways to equal ten"—Provided by publisher.
    ISBN-13: 978-0-7368-5998-1 (hardcover)
    ISBN-10: 0-7368-5998-5 (hardcover)
    ISBN 0-7368-3083-9 (softcover)
[For CIP information, please refer to http:www.loc.gov]

Written by Lisa Trumbauer
Developed by Raindrop Publishing

Editorial Director: Mary Lindeen
Editor: Jennifer VanVoorst
Photo Researcher: Wanda Winch
Adapted Translations: Gloria Ramos
Spanish Language Consultants: Jesús Cervantes, Anita Constantino
Conversion Assistants: Jenny Marks, Laura Manthe

Photo Credits
Cover: DigitalVision; Title Page: Photo 24/Brand X Pictures 24; Page 4: Deirdre Barton/Capstone Press; Page 6: Deirdre Barton/Capstone Press; Page 8: G. K. & Vikki Hart/PhotoDisc; Page 10: Photo courtesy of Jenny Peacocke; Page 12: DigitalVision; Page 14: DigitalVision; Page 16: Steve Mason/PhotoDisc

1 2 3 4 5 6 11 10 09 08 07 06

¿Qué hace diez?

por Lisa Trumbauer

Yellow Umbrella Books
for early readers

4

Una flor aquí,

más nueve flores aquí,
hacen diez.

Tres perritos aquí,

más siete perritos aquí,
hacen diez.

Cinco niños aquí,

más cinco niños aquí,
hacen diez.

¿Qué hace diez aquí?

Índice